The New Wallpaper Book

ROCKPORT

The New Wallpaper Book

IDEAS

FOR

DECORATING

WALLS,

CEILINGS,

& HOME

ACCESSORIES

GLOUCESTER MASSACHUSETTS

ROCKPORT PUBLISHERS

Liz Risney Manning

First published in the United States of America by
Rockport Publishers, Inc.
33 Commercial Street
Gloucester, Massachusetts 01930-5089
Telephone: (978) 282-9590
Facsimile: (978) 283-2742

Distributed to the book trade and art trade
in the United States by
North Light Books, an imprint of
F & W Publications
1507 Dana Avenue
Cincinnati, Ohio 45207
Telephone: (800) 289-0963

Other Distribution by
Rockport Publishers, Inc.
Gloucester, Massachusetts 01930-5089

ISBN 1-56496-544-9

10 9 8 7 6 5 4 3 2 1

Designer: Elastic Design
Illustrator: Sally Lee
Cover Image: Courtesy of Gramercy. For full information
on Gramercy wallcoverings, see page 157.
Photographs for Brunschwig & Fils on pages 45 (bottom),
47, 72 (bottom), and 127 by Alex McLean.

Printed in Hong Kong.

Acknowledgments

The outcome of any successful project is dependent upon the cooperation and generosity of those who contribute. I have been very fortunate. The contribution to *The New Wallpaper Book: Ideas for Decorating Walls, Ceilings, & Home Accessories* has been most rewarding. I would like to thank, in particular, key contacts and significant associates. My sincere gratitude goes to, first and foremost, Rosalie Grattaroti of Rockport Publishers for her inspiration and continual guidance; to the talented staff at Rockport Publishers who worked so diligently on the book, most noteworthy Martha Wetherill, Rebecca Mongeon, and Lynne Havighurst; to Agnes Bourne Studios; to Bob Broadhurst of Barnaby Prints, Inc.; to Murray Douglas and Shirley Kelly of Brunschwig & Fils; to Linda Newman Brown of Eisenhart Wallcoverings Co., to Paula Tranfaglia of Decorating Den; to Victoria Pace of Village and Gramercy (Divisions of FSC Wallcoverings); to Mary Francis Benko and Marjorie Ford of Schumacher Wallcoverings; to Barbara Drabowicz of Thompson & Company on behalf of Seabrook Wallcoverings, Inc.; to Amy Routson and LeRue Brown of York Wallcoverings; to Pat Chapman of Chapman Jones on behalf of Sunworthy Wallcoverings; to Tim Quinn of Chesapeake Wallcoverings; to Nancy Picunko of Sanderson; and to Paul Bosworth of Whittaker & Woods on behalf of Cole & Son, Harlequin, Warner of London, and Zoffany.

In addition, for their support and understanding, I wish to thank my daughter-in-law, Jean Marie Risney who unselfishly gave of her time to help kick off the project; Joe Sterchak of Robert E. Lamb, Inc., an understanding employer who agreed to a four-day work schedule so I could undertake the project; Suzanne and Steve Hynes whose friendship is deeply meaningful in my life; Tina Edlund for her encouragement to make dreams come true; Chopstix, who had a purrr-fect reaction when I read aloud; my two sons whom I love very much, Marc and Benjamin, who believe in me as much as I believe in them; my husband, Michael, my personal archangel who guides and protects me; and lastly, my dad, Edgar Drollette, to whom I dedicate this book. Dad, you always said I could do anything I set my mind to, and I believed you.

Contents

Introduction

When the phone call came from Rosalie Grattaroti, acquisitions editor at Rockport Publishers, it had a *double entendre*. I had submitted a different book idea than one devoted to decorating with wallcoverings, so I was slightly dismayed that my subject had not been selected for development, yet delighted for the opportunity to work with such a prestigious publishing house that catered to architecture, interior design, and graphic arts books. Rosalie equated my background with the experience to author the subject.

With some hesitancy, I made the preliminary phone calls. And what a wonderful reaction! I found the industry to be enthusiastically cooperative and supportive of the project. Within weeks, my office was flooded with transparencies. Phone conversations sounded like the those between good friends. There were no barriers. The objective was clear! Write a book on behalf of all the effort the wallcovering industry has put into the creative ways in which these new wallcoverings are being used.

My personal experience followed the development of the wallcovering itself and its growth of creative uses. I could, and *did*, remember when I brushed the back of a temperamental paper with mix-at-home paste. My memories were enhanced by the stored bundle of leftover pieces from all the rolls of wallpaper I had hung. As I unrolled them, the baby's nursery, the dining room finished just in time for the holiday, the border I created before borders were available for the new kitchen soffit, and even the dark blue paper for an interior windowless bathroom (big mistake) I used on a project finished at four in the morning, all came back in a *déja vu* experience. In addition, ten years of my career had been spent with a paint and wallcovering company. How many wallcovering books came through those doors!

Even though I knew names of many wallcovering companies, the Internet became a good resource for getting to those companies unfamiliar to me, especially those overseas. If I had not had access to this new technology, I would not have found several contributors for the book.

It is my hope that after seeing all of the beautiful wallcovering designs, their creative uses, the inviting rooms, you will realize that the new wallcoverings are a powerful decorating tool with dominant impact. They are today's and tomorrow's promise kept to the interior designers and home decorators around the world.

1

From Wallpaper to Wallcovering

HISTORICALLY, wallpaper was just that—paper to cover the walls. Bearing intricate designs and images, often flavored with a hint of the exotic Far East, these papers were laboriously printed using hand-carved blocks or designs made on silk screens onto which inks were brushed, to create the motifs.

The process was expensive and thus most papers were within the means of only the affluent. As with practically all other types of interior furnishings, the Industrial Revolution introduced methods of mass production. A greater number of rolls could be printed and a wider range of patterns made available at less expense, encouraging the use of wallpaper in middle-class homes—the general public, as it were.

The popularity of wallpaper increased, but drawbacks remained. It was, after all, *paper*; difficult to hang because of a tendency to tear, and easily damaged by grease and soil. Glues were inferior by today's standards, creating uneven adhesion and making the paper difficult to remove.

While advancements were made to overcome these shortcomings, the paint industry was making giant strides in research and development. Beginning around 1940 and through the 1950s, the general public preferred to paint their walls. One reason was, curiously enough, disease prevention. One has only to look at advertisements of that era to see how heavily promoted disinfectants were, and painted walls could be periodically washed with such disinfecting solutions. Wallpaper, on the other hand, was not only old-fashioned but seemed to harbor the possibility of germs and contagion—hardly the sort of thing a modern family wanted on its walls. As the popularity of paint increased, the use of wallpaper decreased.

When, in the 1960s, the approval of wallpaper began once again to rise, it did so with gusto. Suddenly, it seems, interior decorators and homeowners could browse through wallpaper selection books to find a large selection of patterns reflecting contemporary designs, executed in trendy colors. These new wallpapers were coated in vinyl, a type of plastic that offered washability. The technology advanced so that instead of just coating the paper, wallcovering was made completely of vinyl. Public reaction was favorable. These new printed rolls of vinyl afforded not only washable surfaces but elements of design in kitchens and bathrooms. Inspired decorators found the alternative to painted walls that had proved too plain and boring to be used throughout the entire home. Printed murals had a resurgence, while additional contemporary materials became available. To compensate for low lighting in small spaces like powder rooms, reflective Mylars were introduced. These new wall coverings weren't made of paper any more, and frankly "wallpaper" had a dated connotation. *Wallcoverings* seemed to flow into the lexicon—a new word for a fresh concept.

Today, members of the industry, as well as interior designers, rarely use the word *wallpaper*. Many homeowners, however, do—so either word is quite acceptable. Both terms have been used in this book; the choice is based on what seemed most appropriate or understandable.

Types of Wallcoverings

The following is a brief description of the most popular types of wallcoverings.

COURTESY OF BARNABY PRINTS, INC. CUSTOM PRINTING

WASHABLE
wallcovering can withstand occasional sponging with a mild detergent solution. Useful for living room or bedroom.

•

SCRUBBABLE
wallcovering can withstand scrubbing with a brush and a mild detergent solution. Useful for kitchen and bath.

•

ABRASION RESISTANT
refers to its ability to withstand rubbing, scrubbing, or scraping. Useful for hallways.

•

STAIN RESISTANT
describes no appreciable change in appearance after removal of different types of stains such as grease, butter, beverages and so on.

•

COLORFASTNESS
is the attribute of resisting change or loss of color caused by exposure to light. Most of today's wallcoverings are colorfast.

•

PREPASTED
is wallcovering with a backing that has been treated with an adhesive easily activated by water.

PEELABLE
means that the top layer of the wallcovering can be dry-peeled away from its backing. This leaves a film of adhered paper that can be used as a liner for hanging a new wallcovering, or can be removed with water. Peelable wallcoverings are usually paperbacked vinyls.

•

STRIPPABLE
means that the wallcovering can be dry-stripped from the wall, leaving a minimum of paste or adhesive residue, without damage to the wall.

FABRIC-BACKED
has a top layer of vinyl and an undersurface of fiberglass or cheesecloth. Most are scrubbable and usually strippable. These are more moisture and grease resistant than other types and less likely to tear; they're also heavy, so are usually not prepasted. When backed with cheesecloth, it tends to have some texture, which is ideal for hiding surface imperfections. Fiberglass-backed vinyls often have a smoother surface.

•

PAPERBACKED VINYL
has a top layer of vinyl and an undersurface of paper (rather than fabric). It is washable and often peelable. It is lighter than the fabric-backed and usually prepasted.

•

VINYL-COATED PAPER
is wallcovering that has been coated with a thin layer of vinyl. It looks more like paper than vinyl, which adds some sophistication. It can usually withstand light washing. It needs to be handled with care when being hung due to a tendency to tear.

•

SPECIALTY WALLCOVERINGS
include embossed, flocked, and textured wallcoverings, as well as murals, grass cloth, and Mylar.

PRECEDING SPREAD: *Even on rainy days, a kitchen with lemon yellow and white wallpaper gives the feeling of sunshine pouring in.* IMPERIAL WALLCOVERINGS

LEFT: *A yellow accent is picked up by the enamel cups in the cabinet.* VILLAGE

BELOW: *Historical restorations may inspire wallcovering designs. The paper in the background is reminiscent of old pewter and worn tavern tables.* IMPERIAL WALLCOVERINGS

SOLID PAPERS

can be very inexpensive or very costly. They have no vinyl protection, which means cleaning must be done with great care.

•

CUSTOM AND HANDPRINTED WALLCOVERINGS

require attention to detail when lining up the motif of the pattern. Each motif is diligently applied to the paper by skilled craftspeople, using carved blocks or silk screens. Where silk screens are used, the ink is applied to create a different color in the design. The quality of handprinted paper is unmistakable. Handprinted designs may be historical, perhaps even documented, as with the conservation or reproduction of a wallpaper pattern used in a historical building. Or they may be created to coordinate or match the print of a fabric. Internationally recognized design firms such as Brunschwig & Fils and Colefax & Fowler regularly employ handprint wallpaper shops to create their distinctive patterns.

ABOVE: *Large patterns help fill the space nicely in older homes, where ceilings are likely to be high.* IMPERIAL WALLCOVERINGS

ABOVE RIGHT: *A tranquil pattern for a restful room.* GRAMERCY

FACING PAGE: *The interior designer used the principle of unbroken space to visually enlarge this small, charming bedroom.* GRAMERCY

LEFT: *A dynamic continuity occurs when adjoining rooms are decorated with harmonious, not "matching," wallcovering patterns.* VILLAGE

BELOW: *A large wallcovering pattern adds a lively feeling to this elegant dining room.* VILLAGE

FACING PAGE: *In this kitchen area, the pattern used for the lower half of the dining room has been repeated—a repetition the eye perceives as pleasing.* GRAMERCY

FACING PAGE: *Blue and white stripes are ideally suited for the bathroom in this beachside home.* VILLAGE

RIGHT: *Deep-colored patterns create a feeling of coziness in this study. Touches of black and gold in the decor complement this striking wallcovering pattern.* GRAMERCY

LEFT: *The fashion industry provided an inspiration for this timeless wallcovering pattern, which features women dressed in Dior gowns—ideal for a dressing room.* GRAMERCY

BELOW: *Perfectly matched trim enamel is a crisp accent to any wallcovering; in this case, Wedgwood blue was chosen for door, trim, molding, and little round table found at a flea market.* SANDERSON

ABOVE: *Large patterns have a more dramatic effect than small, as evidenced by the designer-chosen wallcovering in this eating area.* GRAMERCY

From Wallpaper to Wallcovering

RIGHT: *Use a favorite piece of furniture, such as this blue-painted chair, for inspiration in choosing wallpaper patterns. The well-balanced floral patterns of this dining room show the type of creative details one can expect when using a professional designer.*
GRAMERCY

FACING PAGE: *A pattern this size is wonderfully proportioned for this gracious living room.* GRAMERCY

From Wallpaper to Wallcovering

ABOVE: *Contrasting colors, such as blue and yellow, create a vibrant dining area.* GRAMERCY

FACING PAGE: *Thoughtfully collected objects stand out against a warm harlequin-patterned paper.* DECORATING DEN INTERIORS

2

Sensational Style

A WELL-DECORATED ROOM with coordinating wallcoverings,
borders, and fabrics is no longer a luxury few can afford, nor need it be
a time-consuming effort of search and despair.

A wonderful world of decorating freedom has emerged. No longer is using stripes and prints together likely to produce raised eyebrows. One can even throw plaid fabrics into the mix. What makes it work? Primarily, color coordination. When the same colors are in the stripe, print, and plaid, interior style *works*.

One need not have the finely honed instincts of an interior designer to create striking style. Wallcovering companies have made coordinating easy by mixing and matching suggested patterns for you. As you leaf through their selection books, you will find colorful pages showing rooms in which coordinating prints have been applied on walls and ceilings, followed by samples of the actual wallcoverings used. These selection books can give an inspiring look at how to work with various patterns. Oftentimes, fabrics that match are available, adding to the wide range of customized interiors one can realize. A local seamstress can produce a stunning window treatment to mix with or match the patterns you select; coordinated comforters and bed linens can be created; and an upholstery shop can revamp existing furniture into stylish "new" pieces by recovering them with a fabric that echoes the pattern used on the walls or elsewhere in the room.

It is possible to create your own coordinated decor. While browsing through wallcovering selection books, look for the same color within the patterns, or colors of different *values* from within the same color family. Value refers to the lightness or darkness of a color achieved by tinting or shading. A *tint* is achieved by adding **white**, while a *shade* is achieved by adding **black** to a given color. For a good example of this concept, take a look at the strips of gradational colors available in paint stores. The lightest tinted color is at the top, while the deepest shaded color is at the bottom. Using a tint and a shade, one as dominant and the other as an accent or trim color, will result in good color coordination. Use the same principle of color value to guide you in selecting wallcovering patterns.

Mixed and matched wallcoverings can be used with one pattern on the upper half of a wall and the other on the lower half with a wooden chair rail or a wallcovering border to separate the patterns. Or use a dominant pattern on three walls with a coordinated pattern on the fourth. A dormered room can be papered with a dark background pattern on its walls and the same pattern, but in reverse (oftentimes available), within the dormers. The lighter reverse background will produce more reflected light.

The Feeling of Color

Here, color is broken down into families based around the same basic hue.

THE *RED* FAMILY

HUES

pink, rose, cardinal, raspberry, burgundy, maroon

CHARACTERISTICS

warmest of all colors, advancing, cheerful, active, stimulating, bold, vital, dramatic, exciting

EFFECT

A red room appears smaller by bringing the background closer; red objects appear larger because red focuses attention; red brings warmth and excitement to a cool room.

PRECAUTION

Too much red is overly exciting.

FAST FACT

A red room stimulates appetite.

·

THE *ORANGE* FAMILY

HUES

peach, coral, pumpkin, copper, terra-cotta, rust, warm brown

CHARACTERISTICS

welcoming, cheerful, warm, glowing, advancing, friendly

EFFECT

Much like the red family but to a lesser degree; in soft tints is a good color mixer; a good choice for kitchens and family rooms.

PRECAUTION

Like red, can be overwhelming if overused.

FAST FACT

Orange rooms tend to make people tire more easily.

THE *YELLOW* FAMILY

HUES

cream, straw, lemon, canary, gold, tan, tobacco

CHARACTERISTICS

warm, luminous, radiant, classic, expansive, accepting

EFFECT

Yellow rooms appear brighter and lighter because of the color's reflective quality; can be used to light up a room without making it feel smaller; a classic kitchen choice.

PRECAUTION

Yellow tints and tones need to be tested under artificial light as they appear different in various kinds of light.

FAST FACT

Babies tend to cry more and children are more argumentative in yellow nurseries than in pink, baby blue, or pale green rooms.

·

THE *GREEN* FAMILY

HUES

mint, lettuce, pea, grass, sea, olive, bottle, forest

CHARACTERISTICS

refreshing, cool, receding, restful

EFFECT

In lighter shades, a room will seem larger because the wall seems further away; brings atmosphere of relaxation to room; important hue where restfulness is important; most friendly with all other colors.

PRECAUTION

May make a room with a northern exposure feel cold.

FAST FACT

Green is least tiring to the eyes, which is the reason accountants' shades and surgeons' traditional scrubs are green.

·

THE *BLUE* FAMILY

HUES

baby, powder, sky, turquoise, royal, navy, midnight

CHARACTERISTICS

coolest of all colors, most receding, much-loved hue, serene

EFFECT

Blue room appears cooler than if painted with a warm hue; makes a room feel more airy and spacious; makes objects look smaller and more distant; makes whites appear more luminescent.

PRECAUTION

Can be depressing in dull shades.

FAST FACT

People associate stability and leadership with the color blue; important documents are often bound in blue.

THE *VIOLET* FAMILY

HUES

orchid, lavender, mauve, violet, purple, plum

CHARACTERISTICS

impressive hue; creates quiet feeling atmosphere

EFFECT

Dark tones make objects appear formal and rich; transitional color—feels cool when mixed with blue and warm when mixed with red; meditative.

PRECAUTION

Strong shades can be overpowering.

FAST FACT

In medieval times, only royalty was allowed to wear purple.

PRECEDING SPREAD: *As minimalism becomes more popular, we are likely to see patterns that fit the look.* IMPERIAL WALLCOVERINGS

ABOVE: *Older homes often have interesting architectural details such as the arched window and the built-in cabinet beside the fireplace. This appropriate wallcovering captures the spirit of the early twentieth century.* GRAMERCY

BELOW: *A traditional foyer sets the tone for a home. Don't be afraid to use rich colors; this red, for example, suggests warmth and cheerfulness.* SCHUMACHER

LEFT: *In this authentic bath, a botanical print wallcovering was used. Botanical prints were popular in the early part of this century. Good reproductions, such as this pedestal sink and footed bathtub, are now available for those wishing to capture the look.* GRAMERCY

BELOW: *A different pattern of wallcovering helps to differentiate the alcove space from the rest of the room.* SEABROOK WALLCOVERINGS

ABOVE: *Although we often associate red with oriental motifs, this blue with a subtle fish design works wonderfully with the decor.*
GRAMERCY

RIGHT: *A very charming eating area with a great deal of coordination. Everything matches to create a harmonious mood.* HARLEQUIN—
DISTRIBUTED BY WHITTAKER & WOODS

FACING PAGE: *This morning glory pattern was a good choice as background to the bird house collection.* SEABROOK WALLCOVERINGS

LEFT: *A simple, Regency-inspired interior in which the crispness of blue and white have been used for a chic effect.* HARLEQUIN—DISTRIBUTED BY WHITTAKER & WOODS

ABOVE: *In this child's room, the polka-dotted headboard was painted to match the whimsical border, in which bears skate around the room.* VILLAGE

ABOVE: *Good coordination creates a charming decor in this attic bedroom retreat. The fabric colors match even though the prints are different.* SANDERSON

ABOVE: *A strong design, but beautifully implemented, in this large and interesting bath.*
GRAMERCY

LEFT: *A great example of a room in which fabrics and wallcoverings match in color but not in pattern. The exception is the window treatment, created from wallcovering-matched fabric.*
GRAMERCY

LEFT: *A boldly coordinated bath that features a sumptuously curtained tub.* DECORATING DEN INTERIORS

BELOW: *A linear look is emphasized by the wallcovering pattern, which complements the furnishings, floor mosaic, and glass panel adjoining the door.* IMPERIAL WALLCOVERINGS

FACING PAGE: *A straightforward woven pattern is a great starting point for a sparse, eclectic interior.* IMPERIAL WALLCOVERINGS

ABOVE AND FACING PAGE: *A retro 1950s look in this loft apartment benefits from a complementary background. The patterns in these two photos demonstrate how well the selections worked.* IMPERIAL WALLCOVERINGS

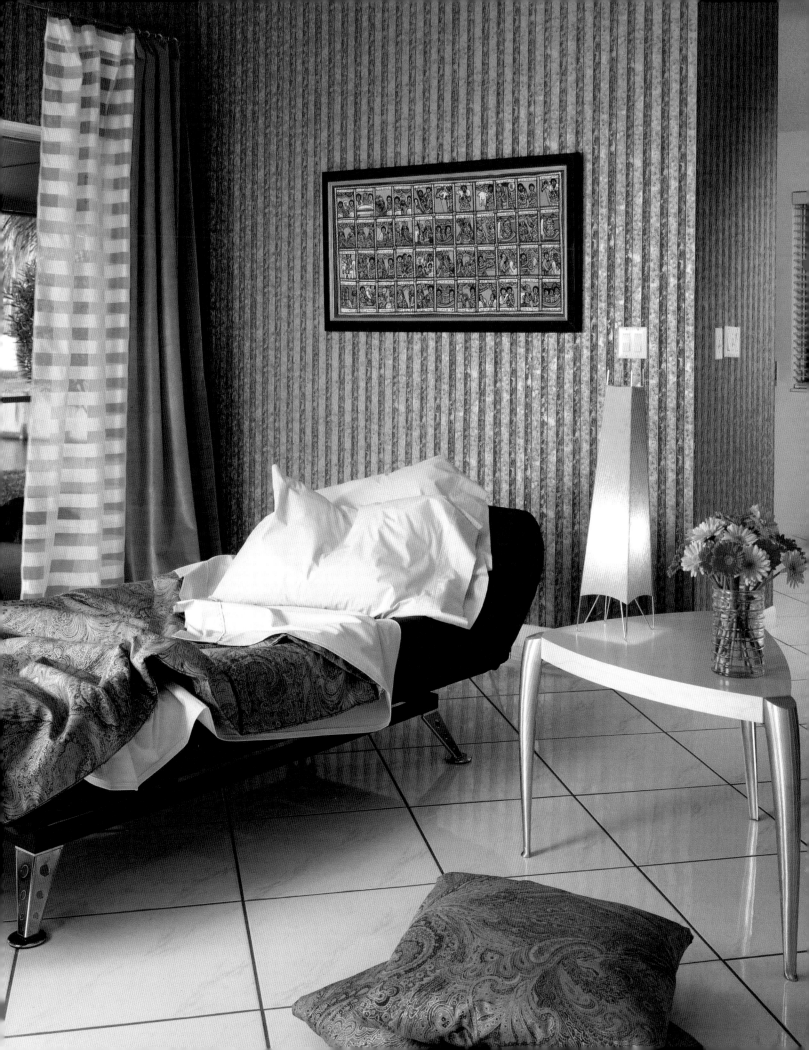

FACING PAGE: *A French country look has been achieved with this simple, yet elegant, striped wallpaper.* IMPERIAL WALLCOVERINGS

RIGHT: *This dining room gloriously combines the tropical with the traditional. The effect is paradoxical—a sort of relaxed grandeur.* GRAMERCY

BELOW: *A Fabergé egg collection print that is nothing less than stunning. By repeating the pattern in fabric details—the chair, ottoman, and pillow—the decorating efforts could be considered flawless.* GRAMERCY

Sensational Style

LEFT: *An ingenious use of wallcovering and borders create an "alcove" in this country design.* DECORATING DEN INTERIORS

BELOW: *A painted pink ceiling softly offsets this lovely French country-style bedroom. The exquisite pattern on paper and fabric is a custom design.* BRUNSCHWIG & FILS

FACING PAGE: *A draped bed and matched fabrics, wallcoverings, and borders combine to create a room of sensationally coor-dinated style.* GRAMERCY

Sensational Style

ABOVE: *A border defines this sweet, pleasantly coordinated nursery.*
DECORATING DEN INTERIORS

RIGHT: *The coordinating fabric to this wallcovering pattern was used for bedding.* SEABROOK WALLCOVERINGS

FACING PAGE: *This comfortable print, used throughout this small room, actually makes the room look larger than if different patterns were used.* BRUNSCHWIG & FILS

ABOVE: *Wallcovering may mimic a painted finish, as in this subtle selection that looks sponge-painted.* DECORATING DEN INTERIORS

RIGHT: *Softness is conveyed by this country-influenced room, from the upholstered screen to the sheer drapes. The starting point is the pale, light-on-light wallcovering.* GRAMERCY

FACING PAGE: *A distinctive border helps create the elegant ease of this room.* SCHUMACHER

LEFT: *A charming pattern for a charming room. This room in a mother-in-law's suite functions as a multipurpose room. What better way to enjoy family activities than in this cheerful setting.* GRAMERCY

FACING PAGE: *An obvious choice for a bathroom, and a fun one as well. The coordinating border in front of the base cabinet is a nice touch.* SEABROOK WALLCOVERINGS

ABOVE: *Soft neutrals create this subued eclectic setting.* DECORATING DEN INTERIORS

FACING PAGE: *This elegant, detailed wallcovering sets up the restrained aesthetic of this perfectly coordinated off-white bedroom.* IMPERIAL WALLCOVERINGS

ABOVE: *This entryway encourages its occupants to be ever ready when it comes to a walkabout. The strong colors in the wide border print of mallards, sunflowers, and pottery stand out against the more subdued striped wallcovering on the wall.* YORK WALLCOVERINGS

RIGHT: *Theme-ing a room refers to repeating the dominant theme. In this case, a backdrop of tied flies used for fly fishing is picked up with the border print and the decorative accessories in the room.* YORK WALLCOVERINGS

FACING PAGE: *Vaulted ceilings are dramatic but this one is made even more so with the use of a simulated cork ceiling. The effect makes the room feel cozier.* YORK WALLCOVERINGS

3

Looking Up: Ceiling Style

TODAY, ceilings are often untapped design areas with which to complement your decor. This has not always been the case. Where once artistic plaster medallions took center stage and richly carved ceiling moldings framed the perimeter of a room, plain blank ceilings, usually white, have become the norm.

As the skills and talents of Old World craftsmen died off, so did the prominence of ceiling details.

The re-introduction of architectural elements in modern materials such as cast resin and vinyl-coated Styrofoam, have inspired wallcovering companies to respond by depicting such details on easily applied wallpaper. Many of today's wallcovering books feature these ceiling medallion and trim patterns, to the delight of the decorator. If the desired medallions are not available, an ingenious decorator can create them by cutting out a motif from a large wallcovering pattern.

When more than a medallion is desired to draw the eye upward, the entire ceiling area can be covered with either the same pattern used on the walls, or a coordinating pattern. When the ceiling is covered with the same pattern, the room will actually appear larger. By downplaying contrast, small areas actually look larger. This is a visual phenomenon decorators often take advantage of. Papering a small bedroom with the same wallcovering pattern on ceiling and walls will make the room appear larger than if the ceiling were painted, or if different patterns had been used above and below the chair rail.

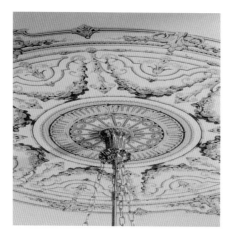

Trim borders can be applied to the perimeter of the ceiling to strengthen visual interest. The corners should be planned so that they adjoin each other at about the same detail in the pattern of the border and cut at a miter. This technique helps to achieve a professional look.

Papering a large ceiling can be intimidating for the do-it-yourselfer. Thoughts of a sticky strip spiraling downward while moving from one end of the room to the other can put a damper on enthusiasm. It is difficult to climb up and down a ladder, pushing it forward while trying to maintain pressure on the ceiling strip being applied. If hanging wall covering on a ceiling is a first attempt, a small bathroom ceiling might prove enough of a challenge; an extra pair of hands and an encouraging word will be welcome additions. Ladders that fold to create a scaffold help ease some of the problems. Of course, when one is looking for effect as opposed to experience, hiring a professional to paper the ceiling is a reasonable option. Papering the ceiling is a decorating technique that adds interior interest all through the house.

Making the Most of Medallions

When a medallion is
desired as a base for an existing chandelier,
its position on the ceiling is easily determined. In a
room without a centered chandelier or light fixture, the
decorator measures the ceiling to find a position equidis-
tant from its side walls. Rectangular rooms are as good a
candidate for a ceiling medallion as square rooms. For
long, narrow ceilings, as in a hall, a series of medallions
can be used. Generally, an odd number such as three or
five is more effective than an even number. It may prove
visually pleasing to use a larger medallion in the center
with smaller ones on either side, or in a case where five
medallions are to be used, to rotate from
small to large to small again.

PRECEDING SPREAD: *A suspended light fixture is greatly enhanced by the large ceiling medallion, suggestive of antique plasterwork once created by skilled craftsmen. Along the ceiling is a diecut medallion border. On the walls, corners are graced with Corinthian columns, adding a Greek Revival flavor to the room.* EISENHART WALLCOVERINGS

ABOVE: *Bathroom ceilings, which are generally smaller than most rooms, can be encouraging to the do-it-yourself paperhanger.* YORK WALLCOVERINGS

FACING PAGE: *This coffered ceiling allowed for a border to be used as an inset. The result is very dramatic.*
EISENHART WALLCOVERINGS

RIGHT: *Here, a plaid pattern perfectly complements the ruggedness of ceiling timber beams.* VILLAGE

Looking Up: Ceiling Style

ABOVE: *A blue and white gingham pattern on the ceiling emphasizes the country feeling in this eating area. The look is completed with the use of matching fabric on the chair cushions.* WARNER WALLCOVERINGS

LEFT: *Painting the slope of the dormer ceiling to match the walls was an option, but papering it continued the pattern flow. The border accentuates its height.* WARNER WALLCOVERINGS

FACING PAGE: *Children love to be totally surrounded by color and images. This young water lover enjoys staring at the manatees swimming beneath the sky canopy.* WARNER WALLCOVERINGS

ABOVE: *This rather masculine effect is achieved with two linear patterns, one on the ceiling and the other on the walls. A shade of red is the dominant hue throughout.* GRAMERCY

LEFT: *A French country look is achieved by using this rich blue paper between the exposed weathered beams of this spacious bath.* GRAMERCY

FACING PAGE: *This evocative room includes a faux finish wallcovering pattern on the ceiling, which provides a mellow candlelit feeling.* GRAMERCY

FACING PAGE: *The plaid ceiling adds a touch of country to this hospitable dining room. The distinctive pattern on the opposite wall was created by stacking a border pattern.* VILLAGE

RIGHT: *The mottled look of this ceiling wallcovering is in keeping with the rich architectural details of the window and moldings.* GRAMERCY

BELOW: *Here is a perfect example of using strong colors to create impact. The austerity a high ceiling can give is totally diminished by the warmth of the deep red-based paper. Building a soffit around its perimeter provides another opportunity to add wonderful detail. By papering between ceiling beams, this farm house detail is accentuated. The whole effect complements the richness of the room's furnishings.* GRAMERCY

ABOVE: *It is not unusual to find small and large sizes of a coordinated motif. Here, the ceiling benefits from the larger, more open scale, while the walls are papered in the more condensed version.* SUNWORTHY WALLCOVERINGS

FACING PAGE: *The ceiling in this older home was beginning to show its age. A liner paper was applied to seal and smooth the surface, then this restful pattern was used to give the ceiling an attractive finish.*
WARNER WALLCOVERINGS

FACING PAGE: *A grass cloth paper was applied to this elegant bed-room ceiling. With grass cloth, real grasses are woven onto a backing, and unlike traditional wallcoverings, the paste is applied to the surface of the ceiling.* GRAMERCY

BELOW: *A classic example of using stripes and checks together, in a fresh blue and white color combination.* SUNWORTHY WALLCOVERINGS

LEFT: *This ceiling pattern is subtle, so as not to distract from the skylight, but to highlight its presence, the border was added. Skylights are appreciated for the ability to brighten a room by shedding natural light.*
EISENHART WALLCOVERINGS

BELOW: *Want the feeling of being sur-rounded by lush green foliage? In this room you would feel like the trees have formed an overhead canopy.* BRUNSCHWIG & FILS

FACING PAGE: *This vaulted ceiling was dramatic but lacked distinction, particularly with the rich, dark green walls. By covering the ceiling with an airy pattern, the room comes into focus.* DECORATING DEN INTERIORS

ABOVE: *This ceiling pattern, with its shaded "dimensional" medallions, resembles an old plaster or pressed-tin ceiling.*
YORK WALLCOVERINGS

FACING PAGE: *The same pattern in blacks and greys gives the medallions more definition. You can see the effect color has by this comparison.* YORK WALLCOVERINGS

ABOVE: *Available now are "corners," which allow you to tie the border together, as in this ceiling corner. This helps overcome the problem of mismatching pattern motifs.* YORK WALLCOVERINGS

FACING PAGE: *A daybed, draped from a papered ceiling, is a dramatic focal point to this room.* YORK WALLCOVERINGS

4

Border Lines

THERE IS a strong correlation between the growth in popularity of the new wallcoverings and the upswing in the market for border patterns. As recently as a decade ago, few border patterns were available; what was available was used largely in place of ceiling moldings or to create a chair rail effect on walls.

Intrepid interior designers, in reaction against the stereotypical, began using borders in unexpected ways. They placed borders at any height, including the top edge of baseboard moldings. They outlined windows to create more definition. They used borders, not in place of rich carved crown moldings, but in addition to them. Two different patterns of borders might be used within the same room. Interior design magazines, quick to pick up on trends, began to focus on these creative border uses, and as consumer demand for new borders exploded, the wallcovering industry responded.

Before their popularity, borders were printed almost as an afterthought. The designs were fairly standard—a rope, a ribbon, a garland of flowers, or a twist of ivy, generic enough to add a decorative touch to most available wallcovering patterns. Today, however, the wallcovering industry tends to design the border *first*; they are following the lead of interior designers, who are likely to choose a border first, use it as a theme, then select a wallcovering pattern to match.

The nonprofessional home decorator has found numerous uses for borders. Those who gravitate toward painting a room will add a border as a decorative touch, admittedly much easier than papering an entire room. Creative do-it-yourselfers who add a faux finish to a paint job with a sponge or use the rag rolling technique, might incorporate a border to disguise the unevenness where the wall meets the ceiling.

Since borders are so often used in rooms that are painted or papered with a nearly solid color design, the use of color and its powerful visual and emotional impact is a tool worthy of understanding. Color has a tremendous influence on our lives. Understanding some basic theories will help you harness the power of color.

There are three primary colors: red, yellow, and blue. When two of these colors are mixed together, they create one of the three secondary colors: orange (red and yellow), green (yellow and blue), and violet (blue and red). These six colors are often arranged on a wheel to help in demonstrating color theory. The red, orange, and yellow half of the wheel feels warm and appears to come forward or advance. The green, blue, and violet hues feel cool and appear to recede.

Select any hue, and its color opposite on the wheel would be called its *complementary* (or contrasting) color: The basic complementary pairs are red and green, orange and blue, yellow and violet. Complementary colors used as the basis for a decorating scheme have a significant impact—imagine red and green side by side. Complementary color schemes need to be used with caution, for it is easy to overdo the effect. Colors that are side by side on the color wheel are referred to as *analogous* (or related) colors. These are the easiest colors to use harmoniously and, therefore, are the most popular. When tints or tones of the same color are used, the scheme is called *monochromatic*.

Finding Your Own Theme

A practice called "theme-ing" is another way of coordinating a room's decor. In this case, the style of a room is produced by using wallcoverings with a dominant motif or a theme, enhanced perhaps with an accentuating border, and then choosing related accessories. Usually the theme reflects the owner's interest. It's amazing that wallcovering companies have managed to design patterns representing so many different hobbies. A well-stocked wallcovering retailer is bound to offer access to prints reflecting *your* interests. This interior features the pineapple, a symbol of hospitality, as a design motif. Though the choice of styles or themes is endless, some popular styles include Asian or international, Victorian, country, and eclectic.

WARNER OF LONDON, DISTRIBUTED BY WHITTAKER & WOODS

PRECEDING SPREAD: *This subtle border enhances the look of solid furnishings.*
GRAMERCY

RIGHT: *The latest borders are diecut or laser cut around the edge of the design. The eye appreciates the graceful curved effect.* VILLAGE

BELOW: *This whimsical border design reflects the spirit of the room. Borders are oftentimes selected first with a wallcovering to match as the secondary consideration.*
IMPERIAL WALLCOVERINGS

LEFT: *The gracefulness of this curved swag and floral border is a dynamic counterbalance to the linear striped pattern on either side of the bed.* VILLAGE

BELOW: *A traditional use of a border, where wall meets ceiling. This pattern helps bring the garden into the kitchen.* GRAMERCY

FACING PAGE: *Sometimes dividing the same pattern used above and below a molding looks static, creating the need for a border.* VILLAGE

ABOVE: *This border can be personalized with the initial of one's surname.* JOLIE PAPIER

FACING PAGE: *In this music room, the border is large and dominant, giving it its rightful sense of importance in the sparsely furnished space.* GRAMERCY

LEFT: *This border gives a beach house bath-room a sun-drenched appeal.*
IMPERIAL WALLCOVERINGS

FACING PAGE: *Kids adore the stimulat-ing primary colors used in this children's pattern.*
SEABROOK WALLCOVERINGS

FACING PAGE: *The nautical theme is a
popular one among sailors. The knot pattern
on the wall under the stairs is used again on the
opposite wall (not shown) where a collection of
pond boats has been hung.* GRAMERCY

ABOVE: *Among quilters and those who love
the country look, patchwork hearts symbolize
love that endures.*
IMPERIAL WALLCOVERINGS

FACING PAGE: *Bedrooms benefit from the more vibrant colors added with wallcoverings. When you wake up in this room, you feel suddenly energized.*
HARLEQUIN—DISTRIBUTED BY
WHITTAKER & WOODS

BELOW: *As the popularity of topiary grows so do prints that contain such specimens. And what to use as a border? It appears this oak leaf and pine bough print does a nice enough job.*
SEABROOK WALLCOVERINGS

RIGHT: *The fruits of the gardener's labor appear in this kitchen. Oftentimes, it is a color within the border that suggests what to use else-where. The countertop takes its cue from the eggplant in the print.* WARNER WALLCOVERINGS

FACING PAGE: *This elephant border is a perfect accompaniment to the hand-carved dining room table and African sculpture.* GRAMERCY

TOP RIGHT: *Look closely and you will see how the border was cut to create individual panels beneath the chair rail.*
EISENHART WALLCOVERINGS

ABOVE: *A shells and starfish border complement a shell collection in this waterfront home.* SEABROOK WALLCOVERINGS

FACING PAGE: *Adjoining the kitchen is this charming dining area where a rustic border has been used above the alcove ceiling and again at a mid-section of the dining room.*
WARNER WALLCOVERINGS

LEFT: *Here the border frames the window and the fireplace wall to add a decorative touch to an already well-appointed bedroom.* EISENHART WALLCOVERINGS

BELOW LEFT: *Molding accentuates the border and its placement above this attractive desk.* WARNER WALLCOVERINGS

FACING PAGE: *Borders that are sculptured resemble the natural hang of a ribbon or fabric swag.* WARNER WALLCOVERINGS

ABOVE: *This is a good example of both a sculptured border and a straight-cut border used together.*
WARNER WALLCOVERINGS

FACING PAGE: *A laser-cut border adds superb detail to this country-influenced bathroom.*
WARNER WALLCOVERINGS

LEFT: *The fabric design inspired the matching border print, used effectively in this room off the center hall.* WARNER OF LONDON—DISTRIBUTED BY WHITTAKER & WOODS

FACING PAGE: *Here, the charm is in the details: The panel effect below the chair rail, the centered fabric design on all parts of the chair covers, the clever window treatment, the green bow over the clock, and the matching swag border create a totally enchanting environment.* WARNER OF LONDON—DISTRIBUTED BY WHITTAKER & WOODS

LEFT: *This large kitchen has been updated by using a stylish, wide border pattern.*
SEABROOK WALLCOVERINGS

BELOW: *A contemporary look can be carried throughout the house by choosing similar patterns.* SEABROOK DESIGNS

FACING PAGE: *A bold pattern helped transform this hallway. Again, this primitive design border can be hung vertically as well as horizontally.*
SEABROOK WALLCOVERINGS

LEFT: *A softly colored border gives an Impressionistic effect in this kitchen.*
SEABROOK WALLCOVERINGS

BELOW: *An architectural detail border has been used in a room where people gather to play afternoon bridge.* YORK WALLCOVERINGS

FACING PAGE: *This avid gardener found the right border for her indoor potting shed.* VILLAGE

ABOVE: *A couple of eating areas in which blue and white colors were used to create a crisp appearance.*
LEFT, VILLAGE; RIGHT, IMPERIAL WALLCOVERINGS

FACING PAGE: *This sculptured border reinforces the traditional look of this room.* WARNER WALLCOVERINGS

LEFT: *A peek into a kitchen, carried through with the same paper used in the dining area. To help set it apart, a matching border was used.* VILLAGE

BELOW: *The reverse treatment, that of using a border in the dining room and not the kitchen, is seen in this setting.* VILLAGE

FACING PAGE: *This large pattern gains restraint from the smaller sized complementary border.* GRAMERCY

LEFT: *A white bathroom is a clean, pure, contemporary choice. This subtle border serves to enhance, not overwhelm.*
IMPERIAL WALLCOVERINGS

BELOW: *This pale border and wallcovering pattern nicely offsets the combination of dark wood and gleaming porcelain.*
GRAMERCY

FACING PAGE: *Floral patterns have always been popular, and give a delightful period feeling to this border.*
SEABROOK WALLCOVERINGS

ABOVE: *For a gardener's kitchen, an herb-patterned border echoes the real thing.*
WARNER WALLCOVERINGS

FACING PAGE: *The viewer's eye can spot the repetitive element in this decor. The bottom of this border has been cut to create realism in this fern motif.* VILLAGE

LEFT: *Another contemporary border—colorful hanging quilt blocks that suggest warm informality.* IMPERIAL WALLCOVERINGS

BELOW: *A great example of how to treat wallcoverings when a trim or molding shifts in height.* SUNWORTHY WALLCOVERINGS

FACING PAGE: *The inspiration for this wallcovering motif is a collection of Staffordshire figures.* HARLEQUIN—
DISTRIBUTED BY WHITTAKER & WOODS

ABOVE: *When borders are used at this height, the eye is automatically lifted when entering the room. In this case, what the eye sees is a collection suggestive of the occupant's interests.*
SUNWORTHY WALLCOVERINGS

A B O V E : *A light and airy interior came from exposing the bare wooden floors, using white paint for the ceiling and trim, and using a decorative border to add detail under the stairs.*

SUNWORTHY WALLCOVERINGS

5

Finishing Touches

JUST AS JEWELRY, a belt, or a hat tilted over one eye adds distinction
to a plain black dress, complementary accessories and creative details add panache
to a room—often the defining difference between good and great decorating.

The eye is quick to catch repeat elements of design; so accessories that match in pattern or color add to the ultimate style of a room. The most obvious choice for capturing this effect with wallcoverings is to use fabric with a matching print for pillows, curtains, tiebacks, and upholstered pieces. A fairly easy approach to adding a matching or coordinating detail to a room is to paper the inside of cabinets or bookshelves within the room. Small pieces of wallcovering are fairly easy to handle. Trimming is the most difficult part; however, the wet paper *gives* as it is fitted to the inside and allows for creasing to mark the excess needing to be cut. The paper can then be pulled away from the surface and trimmed with scissors. Or if it is not too awkward, resort to the traditional method with a straightedge, trimming with a single-sided razor.

Displaying objects to accessorize a room works well and is most effective when they are presented as a collection. For example, five blue bottles of varying sizes, a round blue dish, and one

rectangular blue inkwell grouped together will look far more interesting than any single blue element. Pictures and photos also look best when grouped together. Buy plain, oversized frames and use leftover wallcoverings on the frame border, or use a colored matting to match your walls.

Adding complementary details and accessories to a room creates a cohesive feeling that is pleasing to the eye and makes the room comfortable to be in. A simple approach is to match appropriate colors, textures, and prints. For instance, tiebacks for muslin-type country curtains will catch the eye and reinforce the coordinated effort made. Loosely covering a wastebasket with matching fabric held together with a ribbon is another clever and inexpensive accessory. Small toss pillows add a touch of softness to the decor. There are pillow covers that can be made by simply wrapping and tying fabric around a pillow form. A fabric or craft store will provide patterns for these ideas and more.

Creating Screens

Screens are a particularly easy decorative accessory to make and cover with wallcovering. Solid pieces of smooth wood, or even foamcore framed with wood, can be simply hinged together to create a folding screen. Access to a jigsaw is useful for creating curved screens. Because they are so easy to paper, they can be recovered often.

•

Truly functional accessories, screens help divide space without costly partitions. They provide privacy and create cozy work areas. Screens can be used to hide half-finished projects. Position a small screen to camouflage the look of a black hole when not using your fireplace. Use a shorter screen as a backdrop on a side buffet table.

PRECEDING SPREAD: *The back of a bookcase is an ideal place to add leftover wall-covering. Notice how the china in this hutch is emphasized by papering behind the shelves.*
VILLAGE

ABOVE: *Animal prints add a wild, earthy tone to this bedroom.* SUNWORTHY WALLCOVERINGS

Finishing Touches

LEFT: *The papered background to this nursery room bookshelf turns a dark shelf into playful storage for stuffed animals and toys.* SUNWORTHY WALLCOVERINGS

BELOW: *The folding screen paper picks up the setee's fabric to tie in the decor.* GRAMERCY

FACING PAGE: *In this elegant bedroom, a papered screen covers a dark, empty fireplace with a coordinating floral pattern.* VILLAGE

LEFT: *A covered screen adds a focal point in this bedroom.* VILLAGE

BELOW: *Covered boxes make attractive storage units, especially when the pattern coordinates with the room's wallcovering patterns.* IMPERIAL WALLCOVERINGS

FACING PAGE: *This screen hides a radiator, allows for privacy, and fits in beautifully with the decor.* GRAMERCY

ABOVE: *This spectacular, regal room with an elegantly draped bed is a triumph of matched wallcovering and fabric.* BRUNSCHWIG & FILS

FACING PAGE: *This true-blue, traditional room is lightened with a light, narrow screen.* SUNWORTHY WALLCOVERINGS

ABOVE: *The row-of-houses pattern adds a*
clever touch to the wall side of the shelf.
YORK WALLCOVERINGS

ABOVE: *The dominant ribbon theme of this bathroom is accentuated with the covered boxes on the floor.* YORK WALLCOVERINGS

FACING PAGE: *Preparing to cover lamp-shades and other accessories can be fun. Just a few pieces of favorite wallpaper, and adequate glue and tools, are necessary. To create an adjust-able lamp shade, punch holes in a strip of pleated wallpaper and string cord through the holes.* VILLAGE

When borders are non-directional, they can be used to frame a wall, a window, or to fill the area within architectural moldings used to create panels. The following photographs help you envision the result if you decide to create such an effect.

ABOVE: Here, details—architectural or merely textural—are cleverly combined to create a beckoning window seat. WARNER OF LONDON–DISTRIBUTED BY WHITTAKER & WOODS

FACING PAGE: Perfect symmetry and the restraint of just one orchid make this space stunning. WARNER OF LONDON–DISTRIBUTED BY WHITTAKER & WOODS

Many of the new laser-cut borders allow the decorator to pull apart
sections; virtually all borders have motifs that can be trimmed and cut
apart. By applying pieces of border on door panels and over entrances,
a distinctive découpage look can be achieved.

ABOVE: SUNWORTHY WALLCOVERINGS

FACING PAGE: VILLAGE

RIGHT: *The latest in wallcovering designs are faux architectural details. One can easily create a framed panel effect, which allows for a number of distinctive, professional-looking effects.* EISENHART WALLCOVERINGS

FACING PAGE: *Curved corners, available with some borders, join straight border pieces to create this elegant fireplace panel.*
YORK WALLCOVERINGS

137

LEFT: *A subtle architectural border is echoed in the mirror frame and columns of a hall table.*
YORK WALLCOVERINGS

FACING PAGE: *Bold ionic columns lend importance and elegance to an entrance hall.*
GRAMERCY

6

Tricks of the Trade

HOW TO SELECT AND HANG WALLPAPER LIKE A PRO

For the do-it-yourselfer who is inspired by the images of wallcovering in this book, the following is a guide to decorating your home with some of those beautiful wallcovering designs. Here you will find information on selecting a wallcovering for every room of your home, preparing to hang, hanging the paper, and addressing wallcovering challenges. The range and variety of ideas and tips will make it easier for you to complete your own wallcovering projects with style.

Selecting a wallcovering pattern is a very personal choice, a subjective matter of one's likes and dislikes. While many people find searching out their "likes" exciting, others can find it time-consuming and confusing. Interior designers, schooled in color matching and design interaction, can be well worth their fees to provide such professional advice. A designer-selected pattern, initially dismissed by a homeowner, often becomes a brilliantly successful design element once hung. Use wallcovering patterns to play off special features of a room, such as dormers. Paper a dormered room with a dark background pattern on its walls and a reverse of the same pattern within the dormers. As a result, the lighter reverse background will generate more reflected light.

Particularly for those choosing their own wallcovering, it is essential to follow steps that could be called Matching, Measuring, and Making Sure.

DARK PATTERN ON WALL

MATCHING: Patterns can be plain, resembling a painted finish, have a subtle overall design, or include vertical stripes that produce what is called a "random match." In a random match, there is no design within the pattern that needs to be aligned when hanging these strips. With plaids, checks, foulards, and figures, the overall pattern must be perfectly matched when hanging. The motif will repeat itself at regular intervals. This interval is referred to as a "drop match." The wallcovering selection book will specify the measurement of the drop.

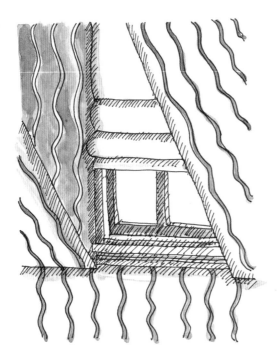

DARK PATTERN ON DORMER

RANDOM MATCH   DROP MATCH

MEASURING: When you are ready to order or purchase your selection, take careful measurements of the room to be papered and allow the retailer to help with the number of rolls needed. They will keep in mind whether your pattern selection is a random match or drop match, the latter requiring more paper as a result of anticipated waste. Count the surfaces that won't be covered: windows, doors, and fireplaces, for example. The square feet or meters of these areas will be deducted from the overall amount needed.

Most U.S. wallcoverings are 18 inches (46 cm) wide and are sold in double rolls, although generally priced in single rolls. Some may be wider but contain shorter lengths. Regardless of the width of the roll, consider there to be 30 usable feet in each U.S. roll, and 8 meters or 24 feet in each European roll.

MAKING SURE: Dye lot match is important. When patterns are produced, a large run is made using the same vat of ink. A popular pattern will be printed repeatedly, each time using a new vat of ink. The colors might change slightly due to pigment saturation of the ink batch, air temperature, humidity of the paper, drying time, or any number of other factors. While this does not affect paper quality nor in any way make it inferior, a color shift could be noticeable. For this reason, it is important to buy the right number of rolls, all bearing the same dye lot numbers, at the start.

A good wallcovering job will last for years with just general care and maintenance. In all probability, you'll tire of the pattern before it actually needs to be replaced.

ABOVE: *Random match pattern.* WARNER

BELOW: *Drop match pattern.* EISENHART

Sampling: The Secret of Successful Style

When selecting a pattern, it's worth ordering a small sample.
Tape it to the wall of the room in which it will be used.

•

The natural, artificial, and reflected light within that particular room will no doubt
appear to change a color. You may find you are not as enamored with the paper's color
or pattern as you were in the wallcovering shop. Hanging a sample will also give you an
opportunity to judge the size of a pattern. Too many times, novice buyers shy away from
large prints, opting for smaller ones. This can turn to regret; although the detail can be
easily discerned on the pages of a wallcovering selection book, it may become lost once
applied to a larger surface. This can be a particularly embarrassing gaffe; for example,
papering a boy's bedroom in white paper with a small red fleur-de-lis pattern can seem
like a great choice—but the paper may "read" not as red and white but pink!

•

Large designs may look overwhelming on a 12" x 24" (30 cm x 61 cm)
page and its drop-match dimensions may seem intimidating. Rest assured, the
former is only a matter of perspective, the latter easily overcome by working from
two different rolls. The lesson to be learned is give yourself an opportunity to
live with a pattern before committing to it. This extra step may save you from a
costly and exasperating mistake.

Preparing to Hang

If you are tempted to hang wallcoverings yourself, do it! As with any project, having the right tools and being properly prepared goes a long way toward keeping a challenging process an enjoyable experience.

Avoid the nightmare of a project started late in the day. Deciding that seven at night is not too late to start hanging a wallcovering can lead to frustration and an unfinished project at midnight. Being tired always seems to create more difficulties than tackling a project fresh and well rested. The best do-it-yourself sequence is to plan the project, strip the old paper, and prepare the wall surface one day, and hang the new wallcovering the next.

Initial planning involves examining a room to determine the least conspicuous spot for starting and stopping, because it is unlikely that the pattern is going to match exactly at that point. A good spot may be a corner, or over the least-noticed doorway where there is only a small amount of paper. Another method is to determine where the focal point of the room is and start there, work to the start/stop point, then return to the first (focal) strip and continue in the other direction. This works well when it is important to center the pattern, particularly when hanging large patterns. In a room with a natural focal point, such as a fireplace, it is important to have a prominent piece of the pattern centered exactly over the mantel.

Although rare, mistakes in the pattern do occur. Wallcovering companies advise inspecting each roll for any imperfections, usually in the print registration. If found, the companies are generally very amenable about exchanging them.

STRIPPING WALLPAPER WITH PUTTY KNIFE

STRIPPING is a major part of the task. If the existing paper is not readily strippable or peel-able, spray the paper with a commercial wallcovering stripper solution, which is faster and cleaner than the homemade recipe of white vinegar and warm water. A small, round serrated scoring tool that creates superficial tracks is a help; it encourages the solution to penetrate. Use a putty knife to get under a loosened piece and, with a large trash can at the ready, tug, pull, or scrape away the old paper, immediately disposing of it so you will not have to pick the sticky pieces off the bottom of your shoes. After stripping, wash the wall with water and vinegar to remove any residual paste. To give trim a fresh appearance, paint it after stripping off the old paper but before applying the new wallcovering.

PREPARING the surface of the wall promotes professional-looking results. Spackle holes left from picture hanging and any dents or imperfections in the wallboard, and lightly sand the entire wall when dry. With new construction, walls must be primed before hanging wallpaper. It is also helpful to size the wall; sizing is a product applied to primed wallboard that dries quickly and provides some "slippage" when positioning the paper. It also speeds up the process of removing the paper when ready to redecorate, because it restricts the absorption of paste into the porous wallboard. Older walls, cracked plaster, and less-than-perfect surfaces benefit from a layer of liner paper as a substrate wallpaper. Liner paper is a plain paper that simply smoothes the surface of the walls.

A FINAL TASK before hanging paper is to establish plumb lines. A plumb line is a straight vertical line used as a reference for aligning the edge of the paper. This can be done with a plumb bob and chalk line, or a long level. It is not advisable to use the edge of the ceiling as your reference point as ceilings are often not truly straight. Plumb lines need to be established at the start point and a couple of inches away from each of the corners in the room.

USING A LONG LEVEL

Hanging the Paper

At last, it is time to hang your new wallcovering. With a drop pattern, when several rolls of paper are needed, plan to work from two rolls—Roll A and Roll B—concurrently. This is a professional trick that is a well-kept secret; the results are perfection.

- Cut your first strip from Roll A and hang it. Line up the next strip from Roll B; expect the first cut on Roll B to produce perhaps as much as 2 feet (0.6 meters) of waste (depending on the amount of drop). From that point on, however, where the cut on Roll A leaves off, that pattern is picked right up by Roll B.

- Another trick of the trade deals with solid color or random match patterns. The color from left to right is likely to differ very slightly; when it is hung, this variation becomes noticeable. Every other strip should be hung top to bottom, with the intervening strips reversed, "top" down and "bottom" up. This will keep like edges aligned with like edges. A subtle herringbone pattern with a slight color shift, when hung without this top-to-bottom matching method, can be very noticeable.

- For a room with an 8-foot (2.4-meter) ceiling, cut a strip about 8' 4" (2.6 meters) long. Loosely rolled, place it in a water-filled trough for the amount of time the manufacturer has recommended. Pull it out gently, unrolling it as you do so, and fold it over onto itself, glue side to glue side, to "book" for a couple of minutes. This booking process activates the paste.

- Using a small stepladder, attach the paper at the top, aligning the edge along an established plumb line. Use a wallcovering tool called a wide brush to smooth out the paper. Work from the center up and then from the center down, smoothing out the air bubbles. There may be an occasion to lift some of the paper and reposition it if it doesn't line up properly or if there is a stubborn bubble. Although some instructions call for piercing air bubbles with

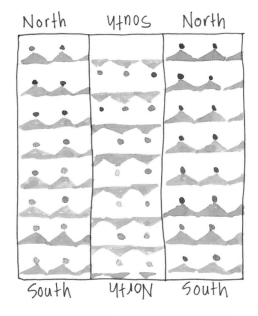

HERRINGBONE PATTERN PAPER
NORTH TO SOUTH—SOUTH TO NORTH

BOOKING THE PAPER

147

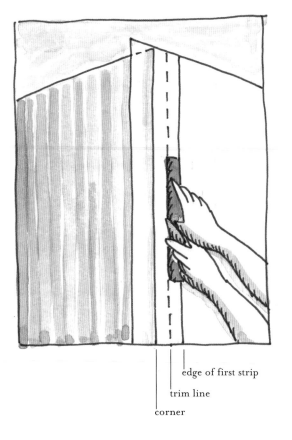

edge of first strip

trim line

corner

DOUBLE CUTTING METHOD

a knife or pin, it is best not to abuse the paper in that way. Use a straightedge in the form of a broadknife to hold the paper at the ceiling or floor molding, and a sharp utility or craft knife along its edge to cut away the extraneous inch or two of paper. It is imperative to always have a razor-sharp cutting tool; anything less will "chew" at the wet paper. A utility or craft knife with a series of snap-off blades is ideal. Break off a new point every two strips.

- Plan the next strip to line up perfectly with the previous strip. Again, with a random match or a small print with a short repeat, this is easy. If the drop match is considerable, resort to the Roll A/Roll B process. It is advisable not to continue wrapping the paper around a corner to any extent. In other words, when you approach an inside or outside corner, plan to cut your strip vertically so that it only wraps past the corner by an inch or two. When you hang the adjoining strip, the edge will probably not be the factory-cut edge. There's a professional technique called "double cutting" that makes the transition in this case nearly flawless.

- Match the next strip of paper, overlapping it by a couple of inches, and with a fresh blade on your knife, use a long straight edge (a metal yardstick is ideal) to trim from top to bottom through both strips. Lift the edge of the top strip to remove the excess of the bottom strip. Reposition the top strip. It will align perfectly.

- Throughout the project, after each strip has been hung, wipe the seam with a weak solution of soapy water to remove any excess paste that might have squeezed out. If left, it will discolor.

- Finally, glance at each wall from an angle. If you see any shiny spots, give them one last wipe to remove any paste you may have missed.

- It is advisable to keep leftover paper in case it gets damaged. If needed, a patch can be made by removing a small area around the damage and replacing it with the exact cut of the pattern.

Challenging Situations

Papering a room can be simple. Unfortunately, not all rooms allow for such simplicity.

- Bathrooms fall into the not-so-simple category. Because of their fixtures, tile, and installed cabinets, there are obstacles that create a challenge to cut around. Where there's a protrusion such as a bathroom tissue holder, adhere the strip and score the paper over the holder by making an *X*, allowing the fixture to punch through.

- Carefully cut away most of the unneeded paper. Smooth the strip on the wall and around the area. Trim along the edge of the fixture as you would along the ceiling, using the broadknife and a razor-sharp blade. Light fixtures and exhaust fans can be handled the same way. You may need to make overlapping *X*s with these larger protrusions. Electrical switches and outlets are treated in the same fashion but require less exactness because a switch plate will cover the cuts.

- Windows and doors offer another challenge. As with fixtures, there is a relatively easy solution. Allow the paper to fall over the frame. Cut away excess, leaving about an inch and a half to be trimmed. Cut a diagonal or miter at the corner, which will allow you to "ease" the paper into place. Trim right up to the frame.

- With more complicated cuts, such as around windowsills where the apron molding is more detailed, take your time and cut around one contour at a time. Rather than use a utility knife on these difficult cuts, use a fingernail to score or crease the outline of the contour on the paper, lift the strip slightly, and trim with cuticle scissors.

TISSUE HOLDER POKING THROUGH
X CUT IN PAPER

TRIMMING AROUND TOP OF
DOOR/WINDOW FRAME

149

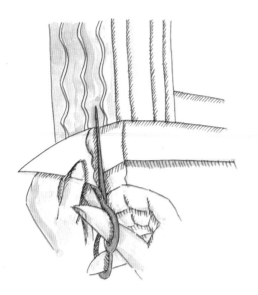

TRIMMING AROUND BOTTOM
OF WINDOWSILL

- When the room is finished, go through scraps of leftover paper to cover electrical outlet covers and switch plates to create a professional finish. Line up the pattern, then cut out a piece slightly larger than the cover. A little *X* needs to be cut where the switch comes through or the holes for an electrical plug are located and its pieces folded back to the other side. Tape can be used to secure these pieces, if it seems the glue's adhesion is not strong enough. With a sharp point, punch the paper where the screws fit through.

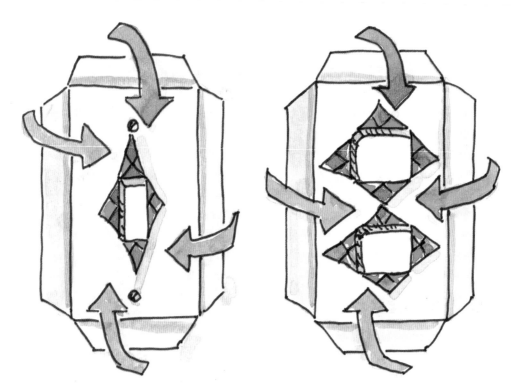

BACK OF SWITCH PLATE AND BACK OF OUTLET COVER

Printing Practices

Whether for borders or wallcoverings, the printing process is interesting in itself. There are four major wallcovering printing processes.

•

SURFACE PRINTING is the same as block printing but in its automated form; a brass roller is etched to produce the design. As a mental illustration, imagine a rose motif. To create definition, the brass between the petals is cut away, as is the area surrounding the flower head. Also cut away is the area around the stem. The veins in the leaf on the stem are etched out to add more realism. The resulting stemmed rose is inked each time the roller is rotated. This roller stamps the pattern on the paper as it is web-fed through the printer.

Surface printing is still the favored process of high-end wallcoverings. The image tends to be a little less exact than with other printing methods, which appeals to those desiring an original look to the motif.

•

Fine mesh screens are used in the *SCREEN PRINTING* process to block out areas not intended to be inked. Employing virtually the same methods used to silkscreen T shirts, the ink is applied to the paper in only the designated area. Using the rose again as an example, the mesh area surrounding the rose is sealed so inks will not penetrate, while the design of the rose on the mesh is left open to allow ink to seep through.

Screen printing allows for more colors to be used than surface printing. After drying, a printed area can be re-inked to create a stronger color or a shadow effect.

•

FLEXOGRAPHIC PRINTING is quite similar to the surface printing method, but the roller in this case is softer, almost like rubber. Thus, the inks in the design are more evenly spread and don't typically carry the effect a hard roller leaves. This process uses less ink, which means finer details can be realized and the paper dries faster.

Decorator stores will be glad to show you the difference between a surface-printed pattern and a flexographic-printed piece. It is likely you will favor one over the other.

•

GRAVURE PROCESS is described as the reverse of both the surface and flexographic processes in that the design is recessed, as opposed to being raised. The pockets of the design on the roller hold the inks. This allows for tonal hues and a virtually unlimited color range. The newer images, which look almost like a painting, take advantage of this process.

Selecting Wallcovering for Every Room of the House

THE LIVING ROOM offers space for a highly personal interpretation—what does "living" mean to you? Do you do a lot of entertaining? Does the music of a piano resonate within this space? Or is it the most active room in the house, a place to watch the evening news, groom the dog, remind the children to do their homework? Irrespective of its daily use, the living room is a place where families gather for special occasions, and the combined aspects of familiarity and formality coexist here.

Living rooms often enjoy the benefit of large windows. Where views are dramatic, a subtle pattern on the walls and ceiling will not steal the show. For gardeners, a floral pattern complements the blossoming landscaping during the growing season and makes up for the lack of it during dormant months. In traditional living rooms, a foulard print creates a nice backdrop. If a living room functions as a family room, a small geometric print can lead a double life, like the classic little black dress that can be dressed up or down. This is a room most likely to benefit from the use of design-matched fabrics; a chair or two upholstered in a fabric that matches the wallcovering can be stunning. In a large living room, a medallion or border perimeter treatment on the ceiling further enlivens the room.

THE KITCHEN is often referred to as the heart of the home. It is here where our daily nourishment is stored, stirred, and served. It is also a room in which a great deal of activity occurs. For this reason, a good scrubbable-type wallcovering should be selected, whether for the ceiling or the walls.

Many wallpaper patterns designed for the kitchen are as richly detailed as a still life. Apples look realistic enough to bite into. Steam seems to rise from loaves of freshly baked bread. Collections of plates look dimensional, owing to trompe l'oeil shadows behind them. Typically, kitchen motifs are small to medium in size, scaled to account for their use between upper and

lower cabinets and in and around appliances, without losing definition. And a gingham or check pattern never looks inappropriate in a kitchen.

A large kitchen ceiling benefits from a pattern that coordinates with that chosen for the walls, while a small Pullman-type kitchen looks larger when the ceiling is papered with the same pattern to create a seamless appearance. For those who prefer painted walls in a kitchen, a dramatic touch can be added by papering its ceiling only.

THE DINING ROOM is a place in which to enjoy good food, fine drink, and stimulating conversation. For that reason, the room naturally leans toward more formality than an eat-in kitchen—a great chance to use large patterns and dramatic colors. Because a chair rail makes sense in a dining room, this is an opportunity to use coordinated patterns above and below the rail. In dining rooms with high ceilings, the intent may be to enjoy the spacious feeling of height but with a welcoming coziness that encourages lingering conversation. By papering the ceiling, this effect can be achieved—the room still feels large, but the overall pattern makes it feel warm and intimate.

THE BEDROOM is a sanctuary, a place to which we retreat: to sleep after the excitement of a wonderful day, to find solace from sadness, to lay in the arms of the person we love, to recover from illness. A room in which we spend a third of our life. Why not paper walls and ceiling in a way that reflects how special the bedroom is? Surround yourself with a pattern that suits and soothes, regardless of your emotional state—one that is not too busy, not too bold, but not too bashful. When covering the ceiling of the bedroom, look for something you can literally stare at for hours. Fact or fiction, it is reported that Oscar Wilde's dying words were "Either this wallpaper has to go or I do."

THE BATHROOM is the room most likely to get papered and repapered frequently. For practical reasons, bathroom walls benefit from the moisture barrier that wallcoverings provide. Papers designed specifically for the bathroom are usually vinyl, although resilient, normal wear and some steam-loosened seams are bound to occur. The average homeowner is likely to replace the bathroom paper every seven years.

Contemporary homes usually contain more than one bathroom, often in space allocated within the interior of the floor plan. As a result, many bathrooms and powder rooms are windowless, and a light, reflective overall color of wallcovering is a good choice; though a powder room can also be papered in dark, rich colors that reinforce a precious feeling.

The powder room (or "half bath"), which doesn't suffer from steam and is most often used by guests, is likely to be papered with an exquisite, expensive pattern—as if this room were a little jewel box. It is an ideal place to use rich, hand-blocked, custom prints (often made available only to the trade) on walls and ceiling.

Ceilings of bathrooms, in which the user intends to enjoy long soaks in the tub, can be enhanced by papering. Much like the bedroom, choose something you really enjoy looking at.

THE DEN OR LIBRARY is usually an informal, functional room. For that reason, wallcoverings that suggest a relaxed and cozy ambience—plaids, deeper colors, faux wood, woven grass—are a timeless choice and make a good backdrop for framed diplomas, certificates of achievement, and collections of family photos.

155

Directory of Wallcovering Companies

This alphabetical list of wallcovering manufacturers is furnished for your convenience. The addresses give the headquarters where you can obtain additional information about their products. Every attempt has been made to provide correct and up-to-date information. However, since addresses, telephone area codes, and Web sites are added or changed, there can be no guarantee the information remains accurate.

Keep in mind that new wallcovering patterns are constantly being introduced to replace others being retired. Should a particular pattern in this book inspire you, make sure that the wallcovering manufacturers have it in stock and available.

Agnes Bourne Studios
2 Henry Street
San Francisco, CA 94103
Phone: 415-626-6883
Fax: 415-626-2489
Web site: www.agnesbourne.com
E-mail: agnesbourne@sirius.com

Agnes Bourne Studios represents manufacturers of classic modern design to the trade only. Anya Larkin is represented in their showroom. Complete interior design services are available.

Barnaby Prints, Inc.
673 Jersey Avenue, P.O. Box 98
Greenwood Lake, NY 10925
Telephone: 914-477-2501
Fax: 914-477-2739
E-mail: 102775.564@
compuserve.com

Barnaby Prints produces custom wallpapers and borders hand printed exclusively for design firms.

Brunschwig & Fils
979 Third Avenue
New York, NY 10022-1234
Telephone: 212-838-7878
Fax: 212-371-3026
Web site: www.brunschwig.com
E-mail: hqr@brunschwig.com

Brunschwig & Fils is an international design studio recognized for their high-end custom-printed wallcoverings, in addition to their interior design services. Their contemporary and historically inspired wallcoverings can be seen at any of their nineteen showrooms located in the U.S., Canada, and the U.K. A recently published book, Brunschwig & Fils Style, *by Murray Douglas, presents a rich portfolio of their design projects.*

Chesapeake Wallcoverings
Corporation
401-H Prince George's Boulevard
Upper Marlboro, MD 20774
Telephone: 800-275-2037
Fax: 800-929-1169
Web site: www.cheswall.com
E-mail: info@cheswall.com

Chesapeake Wallcoverings offers a large selection of popular patterns, many ideal for a country decor. Their Web site functions as a frequently changed showroom.

Cole & Son—Distributed
by Whittaker & Woods
501 Highland Parkway
Smyrna, GA 30082
Telephone: 800-395-8760
Fax: 770-432-6215

Cole & Son's wood block printed wallpapers and hand-prints are sold internationally. Their line includes some of the finest archive wallpapers available.

Cowtan & Tout
Design Studio
979 Third Avenue
New York, NY 10022
Telephone: 212-753-4488
Fax: 212-593-1839

Cowtan & Tout is an international design firm, headquartered in London. Wallcoverings are high-end custom prints, many with matching fabrics. Their design studio in New York is open to the trade.

Decorating Den Interiors
19100 Montgomery Village Avenue
Suite 200
Montgomery Village, MD 20886
Telephone: 800-332-3367
Fax: 301-272-1520
Web site: www.decoratingden.com

Decorating Den offers franchises to decorators, each independently owned and operated. Although not a manufacturer, Decorating Den has established accounts with all the major wallcovering companies, which makes them, in effect, a distributor of a wide range of brands. Wallcoverings, fabrics, furnishings, and decorating services are available throughout the U.S., Canada, and the U.K.

Photos for Decorating Den Interiors credited as follows: p. 26, Terri Ervin and Judith Slaughter, Allied ASID, DDCD; p. 38, top left, photo by D. Randolph Foulds, design by Laura Bowman-Messick and Lisa Tripp Hall; p. 45, top left, photo by Richard W. Green, design by Monique Barnum; p. 46, top left, photo by Bradley Olman, design by Judith Slaughter; p. 49, top, photo by Carolyn Abacheli, design by Tonie Vander Hulst, Allied ASID; p. 52, photo by Jackie Noble Azan, design by Carole Andrews, Anita Wiklem, and Nicolette Zaslow; p. 73, photo by Bradley Olman, design by Judith Slaughter.

Eisenhart Wallcoverings Co.
400 Pine Street P.O. Box 464
Hanover, PA 17331
Telephone: 800-931-WALL
Fax: 717-632-0288

Eisenhart Wallcoverings provides handsome, classically styled wallcoverings, borders, and fabrics available internationally.

Eisenhart's design center calls on a wealth of historic documents that also licenses designs to museums such as the Victoria and Albert Museum in London and the Smithsonian Institution in Washington, D.C.

FSC Wallcoverings
Includes FSC Contract, Gramercy, Greff, Schumacher, Village, Waverly, and Williamsburg.

See Schumacher & Company

Gramercy
79 Madison Avenue
New York, NY 10016
Telephone: 212-213-7795
Fax: 212-213-7640

Gramercy offers affordable, distinctive, transitional, and contemporary wallcoverings and fabrics. The focus is on high style with colors that are intriguing but safe. Designs are rendered with extraordinary beauty and care. Available through most paint and paper stores and home decorating retailers. Licensed collections include Christian Dior.

Greff
79 Madison Avenue
New York, NY 10016
Telephone: 800-988-7775
Web site: www.fsco.com

Self-described as an uptown designer brand, Greff is targeted at the designer trade through Schumacher showrooms. Eighteenth- and nineteenth-century American designs are predominantly featured.

Harlequin—Distributed
by Whittaker & Woods
5100 Highlands Parkway
Smyrna, GA 30082
Telephone: 800-395-8760
Fax: 770-432-6215

Harlequin's contemporary and transitional wallpaper and vinyl wallcovering prints and patterns are sold internationally. Some patterns have matching fabrics available.

Imperial Wallcoverings
23645 Mercantile Road
Beechwood, OH 44122
Telephone: 800-222-5044
Fax: 216-292-3206
Web site: www.imp-wall.com

Imperial wallcoverings are widely distributed and popular with the do-it-yourself market. Patterns are fashionable, with many geared toward the bedroom, bath, and kitchen, and are available through most paint and paper stores, home centers, and retail outlets catering to home furnishings.

Jolie Papier
8000 Cooper Avenue, Building #1
Glendale, NY 11385
Telephone: 718-894-8810
Fax: 718-894-9725

Jolie Papier, Ltd., markets their wallcovering and borders to both the residential and commercial marketplaces. Product classifications include 27" (69 cm) and 54" (137 cm) Type I and II fabric-backed wallcovering. Jolie Papier also produces an upper-end residential hand printed collection. Their brands are sold throughout the U.S., Canada, and the Pacific Rim. Patterns are generally available for four years.

Sanderson
285 Grand Avenue
3 Patriot Center
Englewood, NJ 07631
Telephone: 201-894-8400
Fax: 201-894-8871

Sanderson patterns are stylish, many with coordinating fabrics. Their offices are located in New York, Paris, and London. Sanderson products have been selected for use in the British royal palaces, "by appointment to HM Queen Elizabeth II. Suppliers of Wallpapers, Paints & Fabrics."

Schumacher Wallcoverings
79 Madison Avenue
New York, NY 10016
Telephone: 800-988-7775
Fax: 212-213-7848
Web site: www.fsco.com
E-mail: consumer@fsco.com

Schumacher Wallcoverings is a high-end designer-brand border and wallcovering manufacturer with fabric-driven patterns. Although widely distributed, interior designers often resort to a visit to Schumacher's New York showroom to view the collections. The Schumacher Wallcovering brand operates independently of its sister company brands, Gramercy, Greff (another designer brand), Village, and Waverly.

Seabrook Wallcoverings, Inc.
1325 Farmville Road
Memphis, TN 38122
Telephone: 800-238-9152
Fax: 901-320-3675

Seabrook Wallcoverings manages the design and manufacture of wallcovering collections under the Seabrook Designs brand name, available to consumers and designers nation-wide. They publish Seabrook Journal twice annually for decorating retailers and interior designers, which provides tips, stories, and the introduction of new pattern collections.

Sunworthy Wallcoverings
195 Walker Drive
Brampton, Ontario
Canada LGT 3Z9
Telephone: 905-791-8788
Fax: 905-790-4883
Web site: www.sunworthy.com

Sunworthy wallcoverings are available in solid vinyl, vinyl coated, paintable, and faux finishes. They are widely distributed and popular with the do-it-yourself market. Sunworthy collections are distributed through Sunwall of America in Duluth, Georgia, and are available through most paint and paper stores, home centers, and retail outlets catering to home furnishings.

Village
79 Madison Avenue
New York, NY 10016
Telephone: 800-552-WALL
Fax: 212-213-7640

Village offers a full range of wallcoverings and borders in popular patterns. Half of the design collection is geared toward the bedroom, bath, and kitchen. Many have matching fabrics available. Village is widely distributed and can be found in most paint and paper shops, retail stores that cater to the home decorating market, and selected home centers.

Warner of London—
Distributed by Whittaker & Woods
5100 Highlands Parkway
Smyrna, GA 30082
Telephone: 800-395-8760
Fax: 770-432-6215

Warner of London offers traditional and transitional wallpapers. Some matching fabrics are available. Distribution is international.

Warner Wallcoverings/
The Warner Company
108 South Desplaines Street
Chicago, IL 60661
Telephone: 800-621-1143
Fax: 312-372-9584
Web site: www.thewarnerco@
worldnet.att.net

Warner Wallcoverings offers a good range of styles and types available through most paint and paper stores and home furnishing stores. Many of their borders are laser cut, creating a dimensional look when applied. New products include seasonal Softac adhesive borders, allowing for temporary holiday decor.

Waverly
79 Madison Avenue
New York, NY 10016
Telephone: 800-423-5881
Web site: www.decoratewaverly.com
E-mail: access via web site

Waverly offers a full range of wallcoverings and borders distributed nationwide in wallpaper stores, home centers, and retailers. In addition, a broad selection of coordinating Waverly fabrics and home fashions are sold through their company-owned Waverly Home stores.

Williamsburg by F. Schumacher & Co.
79 Madison Avenue
New York, NY 10016
Telephone: 800-446-9240
E-mail: consumer@fsco.com

A collection of Colonial Williamsburg reproduction prints with matching fabrics is available though Schumacher and marketed by Colonial Williamsburg, Virginia.

York Wallcoverings
750 Linden Avenue
P.O. Box 5166
York, PA 17405-5166
Telephone: 717-846-4456
Fax: 717-843-5624
International Fax: 717-851-0315

York Wallcoverings produces collections using all four of the printing methods described in this book, making for a wide range of patterns and prints. York wallcoverings are sophisticated, stylish, yet current with today's trends. They are widely distributed, available in most paint and paper stores, and home design retail stores.

Zoffany—Distributed by Whittaker & Woods
5100 Highlands Parkway
Smyrna, GA 30082
Telephone: 800-395-8760
Fax: 770-432-6215

Zoffany offers eighteenth- and nineteenth-century reproduction wallcoverings and fabrics. Available are wallpapers, vinyl wallcoverings, and handprints. Some patterns have matching fabrics. Zoffany is sold internationally.

Liz Risney Manning
is an interior designer and former training
manager for a large paint and wallcovering
company. She has conducted classes on how to
use paint and wallcoverings, and has written
many how-to brochures and video scripts on
the subject. She currently works for an
architectural/engineering firm.